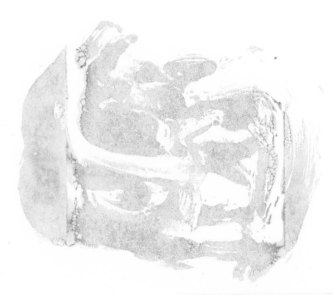

MONEY

AUDREY BRIERS

The Bookwright Press
New York · 1987

Topics

All the words that appear
in **bold** are explained in the
glossary on page 30.

First published in the
United States in 1987 by
The Bookwright Press
387 Park Avenue South
New York, NY 10016

First published in 1985 by
Wayland (Publishers) Ltd
61 Western Road, Hove
East Sussex BN3 1JD

© Copyright 1985 Wayland (Publishers) Ltd

ISBN 0–531–18113–8
Library of Congress Catalog Card Number: 86–71277

Phototypeset by
Kalligraphics Ltd, Redhill, Surrey
Printed in Italy by
G. Canale & C.S.p.A., Turin

Contents

Before Money

If a friend at school has a pen that you like, you might, instead of giving money, offer two pencils in **exchange** for it. If you both agree that one pen is equal in **value** to two pencils, you are happy to trade one for the other. This way of getting what you want is called **barter**. You are bartering.

Thousands of years ago, before the invention of money, everyone had to get food, clothes, and other necessary items by bartering. In those days the **population** of the world was much smaller than it is today. Towns and villages were not very large and people did not have far to go to meet other villagers. If they were not growing enough food for themselves, they could easily find friends who would barter food for something else.

The picture shows a typical barter. If a farmer grew wheat, he could take some of it to a man who kept pigs. The pig-man might want the wheat to make bread for his family. He could offer the farmer a pig in exchange for that wheat. The value would be agreed between them, and both would be happy.

If the farmer found he had too much pork left over, he would have to think again. A piece of cloth might be useful to him. The farmer could take his extra pork to the weaver, who might be glad of a good dinner and be willing to give some cloth in exchange. They would bargain over the amount of pork to be bartered in exchange for the cloth. When more important things were needed, more valuable goods would have to be given.

A Slow Change

Barter was a good system provided it could be carried out on a small scale close to home, and as long as both parties wanted to barter at the same time. If they did not, bartering could prove difficult. So something new began to happen.

In most villages or countries there was often a special item that was valued by everyone. This item was usually scarce and might have been a metal object, a rare stone, or even special beads. A farmer who did not need any pork could still take his wheat to the pig-man if he knew that he could get some of these special items in exchange. The farmer could then go on to another village and swap them for the goods he really wanted. But, if he did not need anything immediately, he could keep the items at home until he wanted to exchange them for something else later on. In this way he could store the value of his wheat.

Tea was highly prized by some of the people in Mongolia, in western Asia, and by people in Russia and China. It was made into bricks, with designs and letters on the sides and was used as a form of money for buying goods. These tea bricks were carried by merchants and traders a long way across the northern part of Asia.

Salt was another valuable commodity. In Ethiopia, in Africa, it was made into blocks of equal size. These blocks had a regular value and were used for trade by the Ethiopians.

On the Yap islands of the South Pacific large rings of stone were used as money. They were difficult to make and were therefore highly valued. Some were very large indeed, up to four meters (thirteen feet) across.

A villager offers some valued items, in exchange for an animal skin.

Many different things were considered to be special, valuable items in different places in the world. Cowries are small, white seashells that are strong and smooth. There are many types of cowrie shells. Those marked with a yellow circle on the back are called "Gold Ring" cowries. One kind of cowrie shell was collected from the coasts around Thailand and Malaysia. Seven hundred years ago, the Venetian traveler, Marco Polo, found them being used there as a form of money.

Cowrie shells were so highly valued that to wear them was seen as a sign of personal wealth and importance.

8

These Ethiopian women have sewn cowrie shells onto the baskets that they carry to market.

Many other countries also valued cowries and used them in exchange. In early times they were used by people in China, India and Africa. South Pacific Islanders made holes in them to put string through, and strings of cowries were carried to market to use as money. Cowries could be stored for years without spoiling, and brought out again when they were needed.

Parts of Africa are rich in natural **ores**, from which good metal can be made. In the area we now call Nigeria, copper and tin were mined and then melted down to remove the dirt. These two metals were mixed together to make another metal, called bronze. Some people in this region knew how to make horseshoe-shaped objects, called manillas, out of copper or bronze.

In parts of West Africa the people valued these manillas, and they were able to use them for trading a long way from home. Manillas could be given one or more at a time and were carried in a bag, or in a basket. The market-traders would take the manillas from their customers in payment for their goods. Then, perhaps, the market-traders would use

In some parts of Nigeria you can still see manillas like these on the left.

the manillas to buy more goods. They found this system so useful that it lasted for hundreds of years. One hundred years ago, manillas were even made in England especially for trade with Africa.

At Kano market, in Nigeria, a trader offers a large pile of cowries and a great variety of manillas for his customers to choose from.

Coins and Paper Money

Why do we use metal for our money? There are many reasons. Metal can be melted, then molded into different shapes, weighed out exactly and divided into pieces. It can also be carried without breaking. These qualities make metal a very convenient material to use for money.

Only when people want something does it have value. If an item is hard to find, or hard to make, it

Melting the metal, and molding and weighing the coins.

usually becomes more valuable. Bright gold is both beautiful and rare. Long ago, in what is now Turkey, the people of Lydia gave gold in exchange for goods. In about 600 B.C., their king, Croesus, had a good idea. He had some of the gold divided into small lumps of equal weight. A design was stamped on each side of every lump to show its value and where it had come from. In spite of their untidy shapes, these stamped and weighed lumps were real coins.

Striking coins to stamp a design into the metal.

About a hundred years later, in Greece, silver was mined around Laurium, near the city-state of Athens, and made into coins. At first these coins were rather rough, but soon the Greeks were making beautiful round coins with a design showing the goddess **Athena**. On the reverse of each one they put an owl, Athena's symbol, so these coins were often called "owls." Other Greek states started to make and carefully stamp their own coins at this time.

The silver "owl" coin, which dates from the fifth century B.C. On the face of the coin Athena wears a helmet, while the reverse side shows the owl, Athena's special symbol.

Philip II, king of
Macedonia c. 359–336 BC
Showing head of Apollo

Julius Caesar, dictator
of Rome 50–44 BC
Showing head of Venus

Henry VI, king of
England 1422–1461
and 1470–1471

Coins provide a fascinating record of each period of history, from ancient to modern.

In ancient times the worth of a coin was determined by the value and weight of the metal from which it was made. The smaller the coin, the less it was worth. The other way to make coins of lower value was to use a cheaper metal. For example, silver is less valuable than gold. Some countries used both metals, so that several silver coins were worth one gold one. Copper or bronze was used for the cheapest coins, many of which were needed to make the value of one silver coin. The idea of making coins from three different metals has continued down to the present day.

Today, metal coins are made by machine, rather than by hand. If you look at your own coins you will see another difference. In the old days the worth of a silver coin equaled the value of the silver it contained. Now, instead of silver, a cheaper silver-colored metal is often used, and coins cost less to make than the value written on them. This is also true of bronze and copper-colored coins. The new metals are better in one way – they are tougher.

There are many stages in the production of a modern coin. These blank coins have been pressed out of a metal sheet, before being stamped.

These modern British coins are made out of bronze, or out of an alloy of copper and nickel, called cupro-nickel.

So the coins in our pockets have this long history behind them. They now come in standard shapes and weights. We can count them up and see that one valuable coin is worth several of less value. Modern coins still have the emblems of their countries stamped on them. This emblem serves as a government guarantee that the coins are their own. It is illegal to copy them.

Most countries now use paper money, called bills, or notes, as well as coins. In the fourteenth century, paper notes were first used as a form of money in China. It was not until the seventeenth century that they began to be used elsewhere. Until then, it was sometimes possible for a merchant to store his wealth with a **goldsmith** who would give him a receipt in exchange. This promised that the goldsmith would give back the gold when it was needed by the owner. If both the goldsmith and the merchant were trusted, this receipt could be used in trade with another person.

A goldsmith counts the earnings of a rich trader.

The Bank of England was founded in 1694. This is the first Bank of England note for £100, which was issued in 1713.

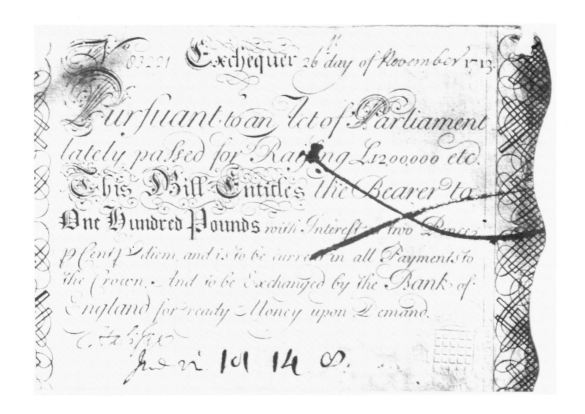

In the eighteenth century, there were small private banks in many countries. These were owned by businessmen who stored money for their customers and could lend money to them. They often had their own banknotes. Banknotes were not just receipts. They were promises from the bank to pay out the customer's money to anyone in exchange for the note.

Using Money Today

Nearly everywhere in the world people now use money in the form of metal coins or paper notes. Today it is possible to change one kind of money into another, so that it can be used more conveniently. Instead of putting your savings in a bag, you can take them to a bank. There your money will be counted and kept safe for you. Your **account** number will keep your money from getting mixed up with someone else's. If you want some money, you can sign a **check** and you will be given what you need from your own account.

On every check is printed the check number, the account number, and the name of the bank.

BAL. FOR'D				DATE	19	$	2771
DEPOSIT							
TOTAL				TO			
THIS CHECK							
OTHER DED.				FOR			
BAL. FOR'D							

2771

ALEXANDRIA, VIRGINIA 22313

19 ___ 68-424
560 29

Pay to the Order of _____ $ _____

_____ *Dollars*

1st AMERICAN
FIRST AMERICAN BANK OF VIRGINIA
McLEAN, VIRGINIA 22102

memo _____

⑈⑆056004241⑈ 0⑈66 14 817⑈⑈

You can use your bank to pay your bills from the money in your account. If you give storekeepers checks for the goods that you buy, they can get the money from your bank with it. The storekeeper may telephone your bank before giving you your purchase, to find out if you have enough money in your account to pay for it. If you wish to travel abroad you can buy some travelers checks at your bank. You can change these into the coins and notes of the country you are visiting, once you have arrived there. Travelers checks provide a convenient way to keep your money safe.

These are travelers checks, which are used to buy foreign currency when you are abroad.

Credit cards and **charge cards** are often used by people who do not want to pay for their goods all at once. If they trust you, banks or other credit companies will give you a plastic card with your name and number printed on it, and agree to pay the storekeeper for the goods you buy with the card. Later, you must pay back the money you owe to the bank or credit company, giving them some extra money, called **interest**, for their help. This way of buying may, therefore, cost you more in the long run.

Credit cards and charge cards are very convenient to use. Each card-holder is given a spending limit based upon his or her income.

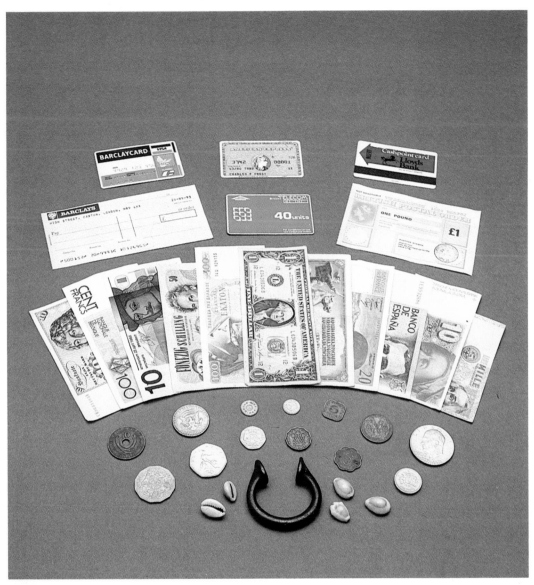

Money has taken many forms during its long history, from the cowries and manillas of earliest times, to the bills, notes, coins, checks, and credit cards that are used today. It is possible that these too will disappear, as new forms of money are introduced into modern society.

Money Around the World

Most countries design and name their own money to distinguish it from that of other countries. For example, in Spain people use only pesetas, while in Denmark they use kroner. In Britain there are pounds and pence, one hundred pence having the same value as one pound. In the United States, one hundred cents are equal to one dollar.

The variety of design in modern money is shown by these examples from around the world.

A couple check the "rate-of-exchange" board at a travel agency before they go on vacation.

When you visit a foreign country, you must use its own money to buy goods there. You will need to buy its coins and notes with your own. You can do this at a bank, or a **bureau de change**, or perhaps at a travel agency. The price of another country's money, which is called the "rate of exchange," is not always the same. When a country is doing well, the price of its money goes up. People then want to buy it because it is highly valued. The price can go down when times are not so good. You must remember to ask about the rate of exchange before you go off on your travels.

Here are some examples of what you could get for one hundred American dollars on January 2, 1980:

100 U.S. dollars = 402 French francs
100 U.S. dollars = 45 British pounds
100 U.S. dollars = 90 Australian dollars.

Five years later, on January 2, 1985, we saw that:

100 U.S. dollars = 970 French francs
100 U.S. dollars = 97 British pounds
100 U.S. dollars = 122 Australian dollars.

If you go to a bank, you can ask what the rate of exchange is today.

Between January 2, 1980 and January 2, 1985, the value of the American dollar rose sharply against both British and Australian currencies.

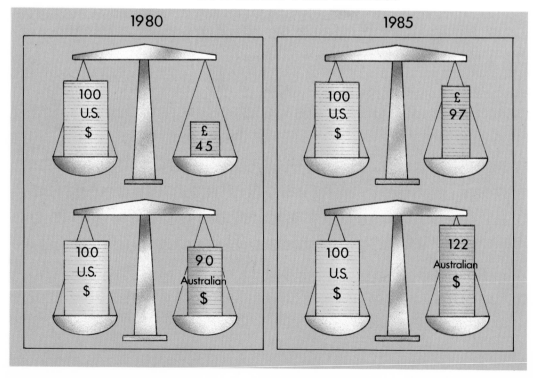

Each country around the world has its own currency, which is given a special name. As you can see, it is common for each currency to be divided into two standard units.

United States	1 Dollar	=	100 cents
France	1 Franc	=	100 centimes
Great Britain	1 Pound	=	100 pence
Australia	1 Dollar	=	100 cents
Holland	1 Guilder	=	100 cents
Canada	1 Dollar	=	100 cents
U.S.S.R.	1 Rouble	=	100 kopeks
Nigeria	1 Naira	=	100 kobos
Panama	1 Balboa	=	100 centesimos
New Zealand	1 Dollar	=	100 cents
South Africa	1 Rand	=	100 cents
Egypt	1 Pound	=	100 piastres
West Germany	1 Mark	=	100 pfennigs
India	1 Rupee	=	100 paisas
Jamaica	1 Dollar	=	100 cents
Tunisia	1 Franc	=	100 centimes
Thailand	1 Baht	=	100 satangs
Switzerland	1 Franc	=	100 centimes
Portugal	1 Escudo	=	100 centavos
Malta	1 Pound	=	100 cents
Finland	1 Markka	=	100 pennia
Czechoslovakia	1 Koruna	=	100 halers
Belgium	1 Franc	=	100 centimes
Argentina	1 Peso	=	100 centavos
Haiti	1 Gourde	=	100 cents
Israel	1 Pound	=	100 agorot

Using Money in the Future

Here are some of the ideas being considered for future use that will allow you to pay without handling money. Many better ways of using money may yet be invented. Can you think of one?

A special card carrying a microchip will enable a storekeeper to check on your identity and ability to pay, and allow immediate payment from your bank account.

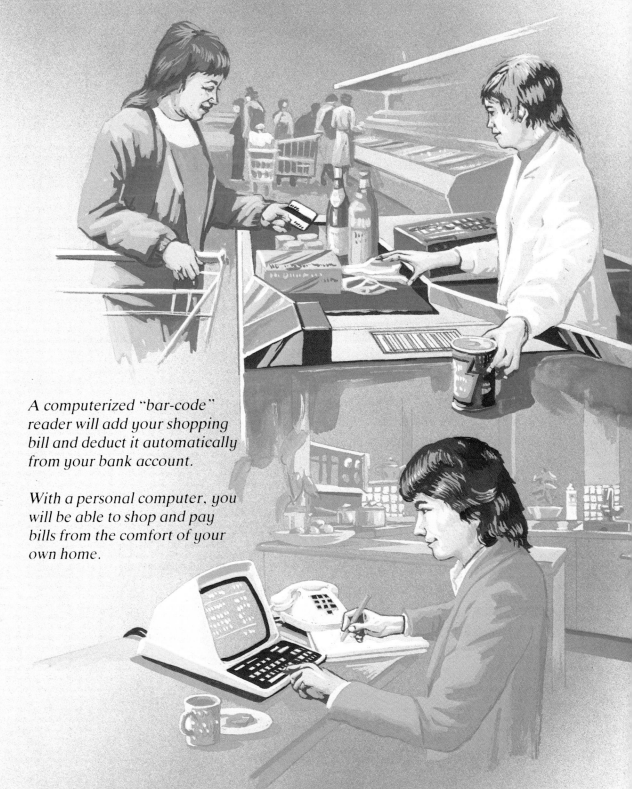

A computerized "bar-code" reader will add your shopping bill and deduct it automatically from your bank account.

With a personal computer, you will be able to shop and pay bills from the comfort of your own home.

Glossary

Account A sum of money held at a bank for convenience and safety – money can be paid into the account or taken out, according to your needs.

Athena Mythical Greek goddess of wisdom and practical skills.

Barter To exchange one sort of product for another, having first agreed on a value for both.

Bureau de change A French term for a place where people exchange one country's money for that of another.

Charge card Like a credit card except that any amount owed is paid in full at the end of each month and no interest is charged.

Credit card A plastic card that allows goods to be bought without immediate payment. The amount owed to the credit company, plus an interest charge, is paid back, sometimes over a number of months.

Check A special paper form, issued by a bank, which allows you to pay money to someone out of your bank account without handling notes or coins.

Exchange To give something in return for another item.

Goldsmith A maker of gold objects, who would also buy and sell gold.

Interest A sum of money paid, in addition to the original amount of the loan, by someone who borrows money.

Ore A mineral that is mined and processed to make a metal (for example, iron ore).

Population The number of people living in a certain place or area, such as a town or country.

Value The amount an object is considered to be worth.

Books to Read

Cantwell, Lois. *Money and Banking.* New York: Franklin Watts, 1984.

Cohen, Daniel. *Gold: The Fascinating Study of the Noble Metal Through the Ages.* New York: M. Evans, 1976.

Fitzgibbon, Dan. *All about Your Money.* New York: Atheneum, 1984.

Fodor, R.V. *Nickels, Dimes, and Dollars: How Currency Works.* New York: Morrow, 1980.

Kyte, Kathy S. *The Kids' Complete Guide to Money.* New York: Knopf, 1984.

Meshorer, Ya'akov. *Coins of the Ancient World.* Minneapolis, MN: Lerner Publications, 1975.

Piltch, Benjamin, and Peter Smergut. *Money Matters.* Bellmore, NY: Skyview Publishing, 1981.

Index

Picture Acknowledgments

Camerapix Hutchison Library, 8, 9, 10, 11; Julian Moss (Moss Photographics), 17, 21, 22, 23; PHOTRI, 20; The Royal Mint, 16; Thomas Cook Ltd, 25; Wayland Picture Library, 18, 19; ZEFA, 24; All artwork is by Malcolm Walker; The publisher would like to gratefully acknowledge the assistance of the following in the production of this book; American Express; The Bank of England; Barclays Bank PLC; Diners Club Ltd; National Westminster Bank PLC; The Royal Mint; Thomas Cook Ltd.